# – The Drummer Boy

Written by **Calie Schmidt** • Illustrated by **Alycia Pace**

CFI • An imprint of Cedar Fort, Inc. • Springville, Utah

A long time ago in a land far away

Lived a hardworking boy
who had no time to play.

He had no trinkets,
no baubles, no toy.

His father was a shepherd,
and he was his boy.

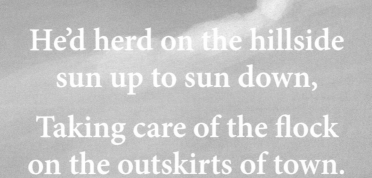

He'd herd on the hillside
sun up to sun down,

Taking care of the flock
on the outskirts of town.

Since he was knee-high
Father taught him the skills

That were needed to shepherd
on the vast, lonely hills.

One day they went to the village to buy,
Selling their wool to trade for supplies.

The market had booths
full of wonderful things,

Dried herbs, fancy clothes,
instruments with strings.

Contraptions that clanged
and some that would click.

But his favorite was a drum,
just his size, with two sticks.

He longed for that drum,
he couldn't deny,

But they were quite poor,
so he sadly walked by.

Exhausted from town,
at home washed and fed,

He kissed his mom,
climbed the loft to his bed.

Then he saw something there as he got to the top—
That beautiful drum that he loved from the shop!

From that day on, the boy roamed the grassland,
Had his drum on his side and two sticks in his hand.

Every day he would play the most beautiful beats,
The shepherds loved to hear, and even the sheep.

After many days came a family ragged and worn,
Aware that their child was soon to be born.

No room in town, no place they could stay,
A kindly innkeeper showed them the way.

In a stable he shared with a sheepherder poor,
They gathered up straw, made a bed on the floor.

That night through
his window
he saw a great light.

A star like no other,
stunningly bright!

It lit up the darkness,
it lit up the manger

Announcing the royalty
of a new little stranger.


As he stared at the wonder
that lit up the sky,

There came the sweet sound
of an innocent cry.

The shepherd boy
knew the man
and his wife

Had little to offer
this new sacred life.

The boy looked around—
was there one special toy?

Precious enough
for this new baby boy?

He knew from the stories what was to come.
Could this be the King? God's chosen Son?

Taking his drum up, he hurried outside.
All creatures stood silent as the little one cried.

Angels were singing.
Other shepherds came near.

He knew with no doubt
that the Savior was here.

Approaching the stable, he fell to his knees
And offered his drum to the new family.

"It's all that I have, and all I can give.

The marks, bumps, and scratches
I hope you'll forgive.

I know that God's Son
deserves so much more."

Then carefully he laid
his drum on the floor.

Mary smiled at the sight
of the boy at her feet.

"I've heard you play that beautiful beat.


Please keep the drum.
Share your talent instead."

So he lifted the strap, put it over his head.

His cadence was soft
among the cattle and sheep

As the Lamb of God
fell gently to sleep.

To Paul. Thank you for challenging me,
pushing me, and loving me.
—Calie

Dedicated to my little family and my parents,
who always encouraged me to pursue my dreams.
—Alycia

Text © 2020 Calie Schmidt
Illustrations © 2020 Alycia Pace
All rights reserved.

No part of this book may be reproduced in any form whatsoever, whether by graphic, visual, electronic, film, microfilm, tape recording, or any other means, without prior written permission of the publisher, except in the case of brief passages embodied in critical reviews and articles.

This is not an official publication of The Church of Jesus Christ of Latter-day Saints. The opinions and views expressed herein belong solely to the author and do not necessarily represent the opinions or views of Cedar Fort, Inc. Permission for the use of sources, graphics, and photos is also solely the responsibility of the author.

ISBN 13: 978-1-4621-4020-6

Published by CFI, an imprint of Cedar Fort, Inc.
2373 W. 700 S., Springville, UT 84663
Distributed by Cedar Fort, Inc., www.cedarfort.com

Library of Congress Control Number: 2019932866

Cover design and typesetting by Shawnda T. Craig
Cover design © 2020 Cedar Fort, Inc.
Edited by Kaitlin Barwick

Printed in the United States of America

10 9 8 7 6 5 4 3 2 1

Printed on acid-free paper